Ralph Vaughan Will[iams]

THE EARLY WORKS

Piano Quintet in C minor

(1903)

FOR VIOLIN, VIOLA, CELLO,
DOUBLE BASS AND PIANO

FABER _ff_ MUSIC

Duration: *c.*30 minutes

The Piano Quintet in C minor is recorded by The Nash Ensemble
on the 2-CD album from Hyperion
'Ralph Vaughan Williams: The Early Chamber Music' CDA67381/2

To buy Faber Music publications or to find out about the full range of titles available
please contact your local retailer or Faber Music sales enquiries:

Faber Music Ltd, Burnt Mill, Elizabeth Way, Harlow CM20 2HX
Tel: +44 (0)1279 82 89 82   Fax: +44 (0)1279 82 89 83
sales@fabermusic.com   fabermusic.com

INTRODUCTORY NOTE

By the time he came to compose this three-movement Piano Quintet in 1903, Vaughan Williams had written four of his most famous songs, *Linden Lea*, *Orpheus with his lute*, *Silent Noon* and *Whither must I wander?*, as well as some short orchestral works and a cantata *Willow-Wood* to words by Dante Gabriel Rossetti. The score of the Quintet, written for the same combination as Schubert's 'Trout' Quintet, shows heavy revision. It was completed on 27 October 1903, revised on 29 August 1904 and further revised on 28 September 1905. The first performance was on 14 December 1905 at the Aeolian Hall, London, given by distinguished musicians of the day: Louis Zimmerman (violin), Alfred Hobday (viola), Paul Ludwig (cello), Claude Hobday (double bass) and Richard Epstein (piano). Presumably other performances followed, but the last known performance before the work was withdrawn was on 8 June 1918. We may suspect, though, that it was not completely disowned and forgotten by its composer because, in 1954, he raided its *finale* for the theme of the *variations-finale* of his Violin Sonata. The first modern performance was given by the RCM Chamber Ensemble at the Royal College of Music, London, on 19 November 1999 in association with the conference 'Vaughan Williams in a New Century'.

The autograph manuscript was among the large collection presented to the British Library by Ursula Vaughan Williams after her husband's death in 1958. The unpublished early works carried an embargo forbidding performance, in accordance with the composer's wishes. But after 40 years, in consultation with her advisers and in view of the interest being expressed in the music Vaughan Williams wrote before about 1908, she agreed to the publication and performance of certain selected works. This Piano Quintet has been prepared for publication by Bernard Benoliel, project controller and editorial consultant, in collaboration with the editorial staff of Faber Music.

Michael Kennedy

EDITORIAL NOTE

The source of this publication is the composer's autograph manuscript score in the British Library, which is headed 'Quintett / for Pianoforte, Violin, Viola, Violoncello and Contrabass / in C minor'. Heavy revision of the work is shown by liberal crossing out and rewriting, particularly in the first and last movements.

Throughout the publication, phrasing and dynamics have been tacitly corrected for consistency, though different slurring in the strings for certain repeated passages has been deliberately maintained. Accidentals have been tacitly added where necessary. The marking 'solo' to passages for particular instruments in the MS, invariably indicating a principal theme but not applied consistently, has been omitted throughout. The composer has included for the double bass some lower octave notes (several E♭s and one D) with the upper octave as an ossia, and to take advantage of the modern extension down to C, further lower octave notes have been added where appropriate with the upper octave ossia indicated by small notes in brackets. These and other significant editorial adjustments are as follows:

I Bar 68, pno—*Ped* omitted; bar 99, db—lower octave added; bars 139–41, strings—slurs are thus in MS but with pencilled alternative slurs over barline as in bars 298–300 (similar pencilled slurs over barline also in bars 145–7); bar 181—MS has *Tempo Imo - largamente*; bars 226 and 279–82, db—lower octave added; bar 336, pno, RH, 3rd note—D in MS; bar 342, pno, RH, last note—upper note C in MS; bar 353, db—lower octave added

II Bar 55, pno, LH—G (third higher) in MS; bar 136, vla, 2nd beat—C D chord in MS; bar 158—*a tempo* added

III Bars 38–40, db—lower octave added; bar 41, db—cue-sized low ♪A + rests pencilled in MS are omitted; bar 49, vla—3/4 added to match notation of this bar; bars 55–58, vla—re-notated from 9/8; bar 59, strings—MS has faint ink *p* in vln only; bar 67, pno—*tre corde* added; bar 113, pno, RH, last beat—♭ to F omitted; bar 120, pno, RH, 2nd beat—bottom note A in MS; bars 123–34—pno heavily corrected, indistinct in places; bar 127, vla, last beat—indistinct 4-note chord in MS replaced by 2-note chord; bar 139, pno—this bar revised several times, MS has D A in same rhythm but alternative A D reading seems preferable; bar 145, vln and vla—*p* added; bar 163, vla, 1st note—possibly ♪ in MS; bar 244, db—lower octave added

Piano Quintet in C minor

(1903)

Ralph Vaughan Williams
(1872-1958)

I

18

K Tempo I (Allegro con fuoco)

K Tempo I (Allegro con fuoco)

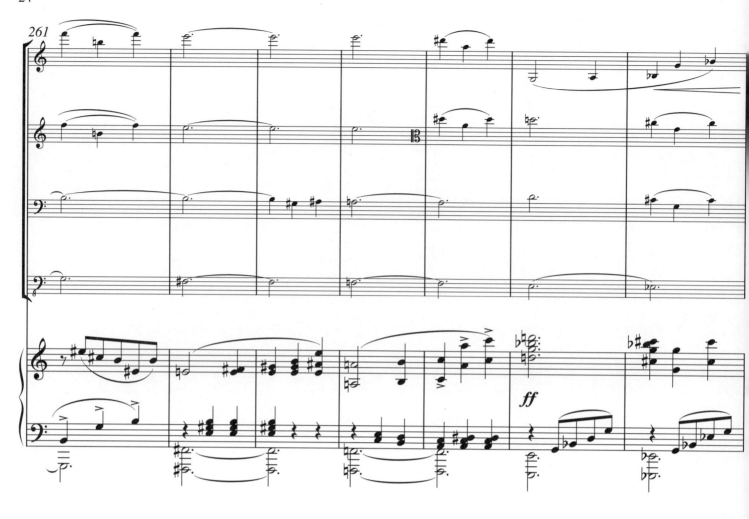

stringendo Q **Poco più mosso** ♩. = 100

stringendo Q **Poco più mosso** ♩. = 100

26

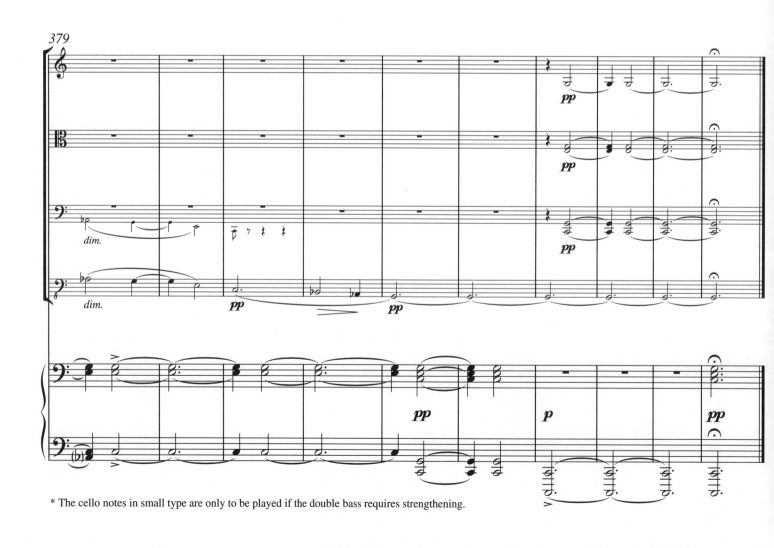

* The cello notes in small type are only to be played if the double bass requires strengthening.

II

poco più mosso

poco più mosso

ancora animando

ancora animando

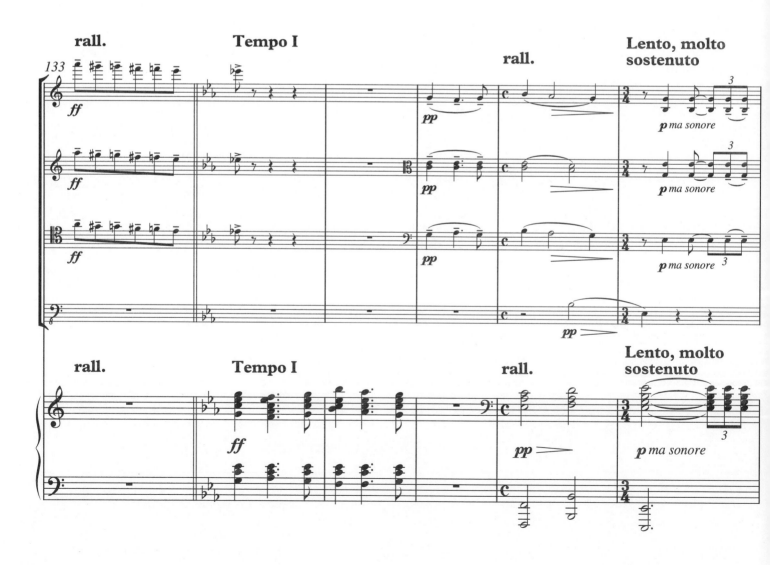

151

(accompany cello)

pochino smorz.

a tempo

155

pochino smorz.

a tempo

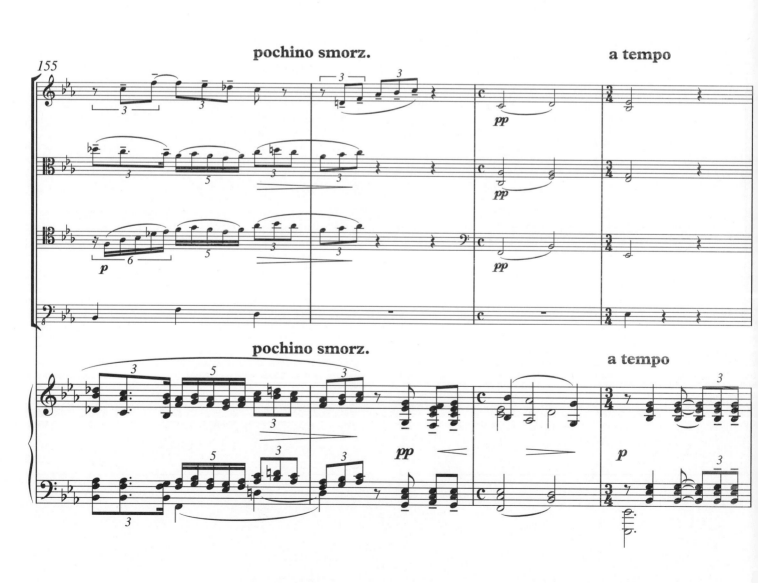

III Fantasia (quasi variazioni)

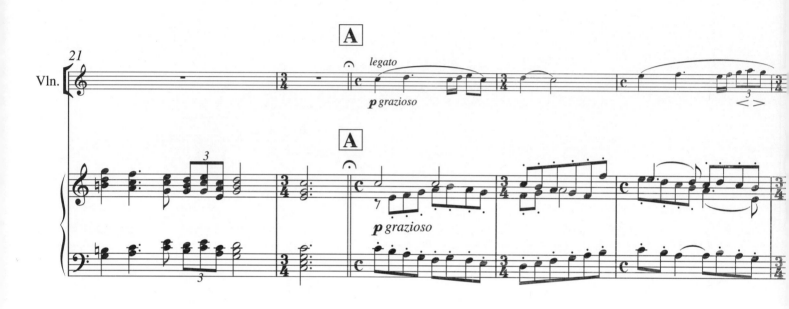

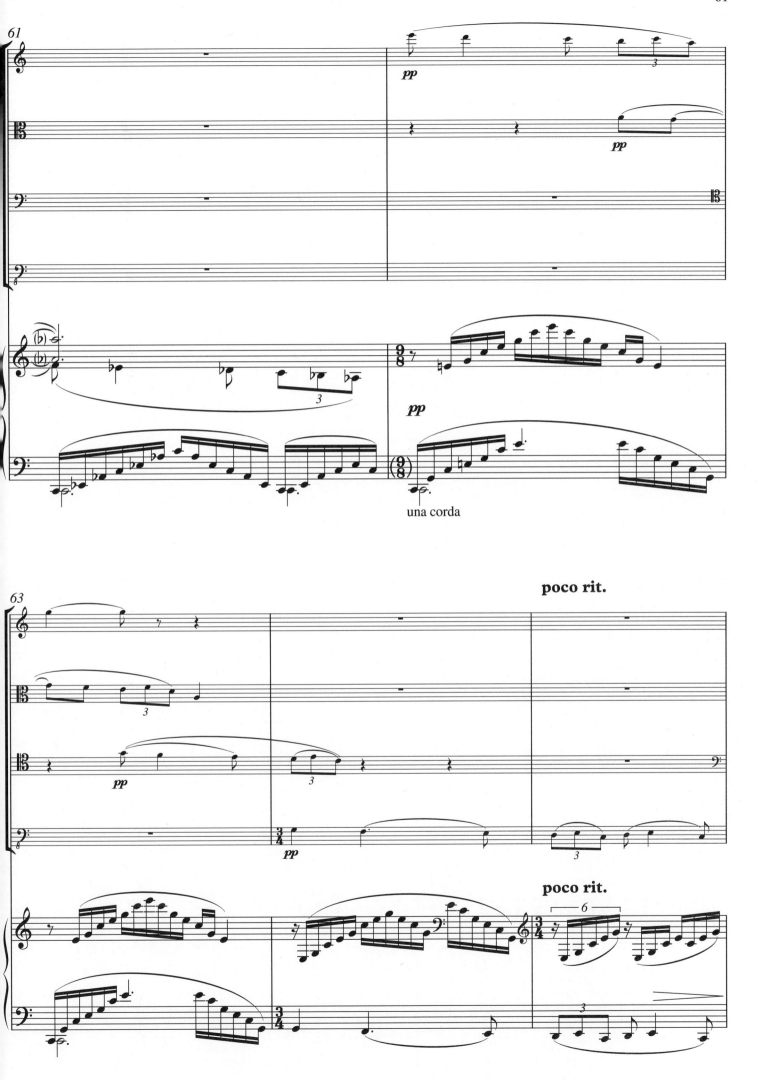

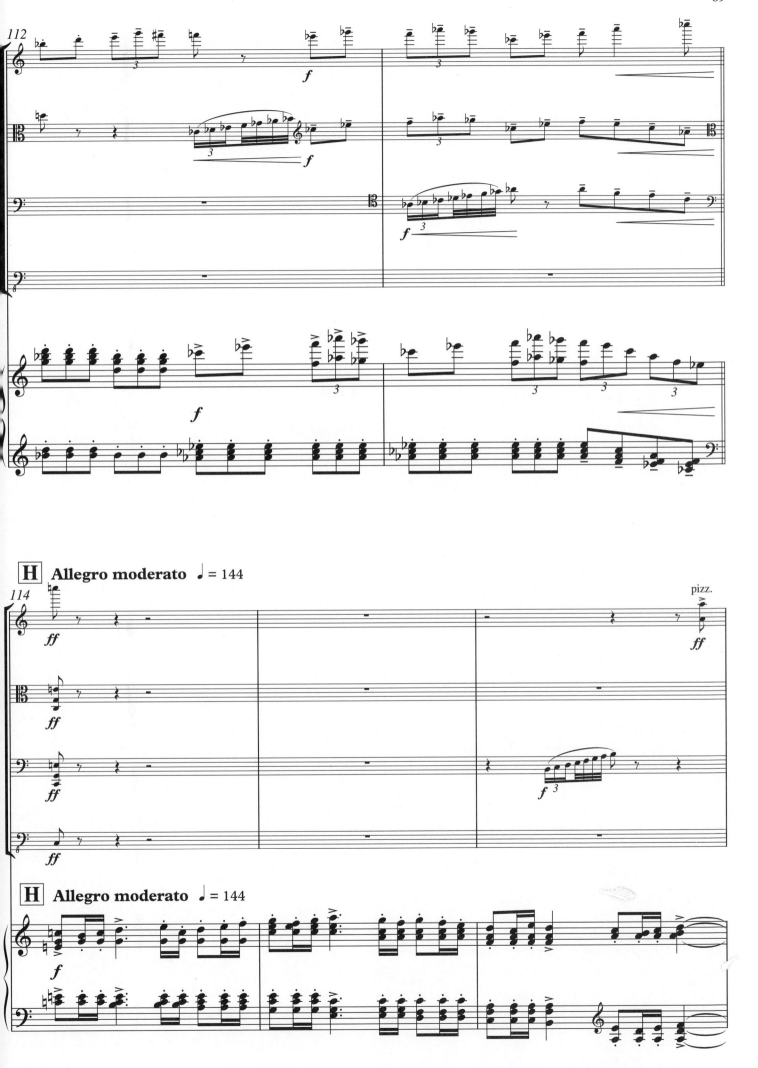

H **Allegro moderato** ♩ = 144

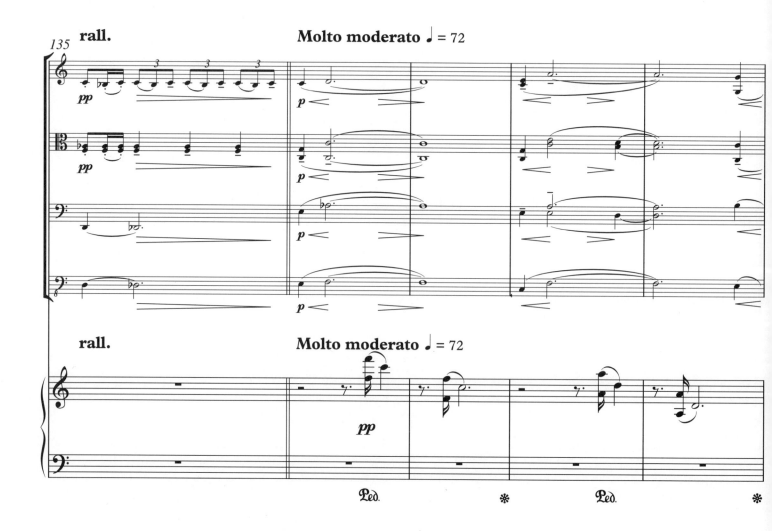

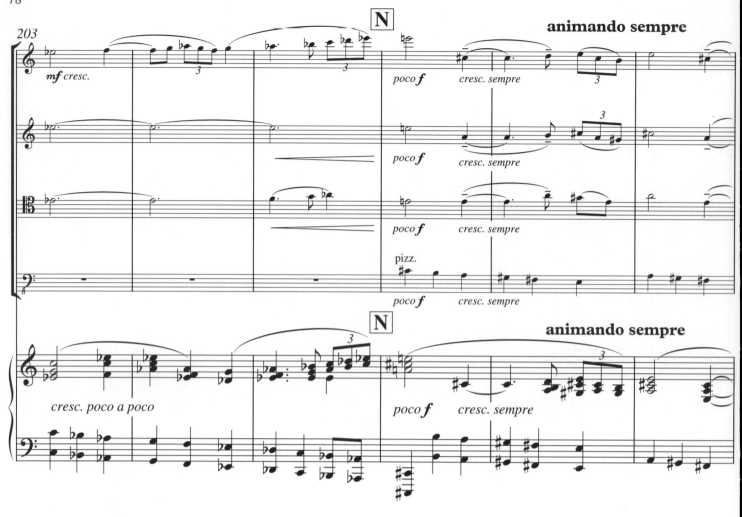

rall. al fine

rall. al fine

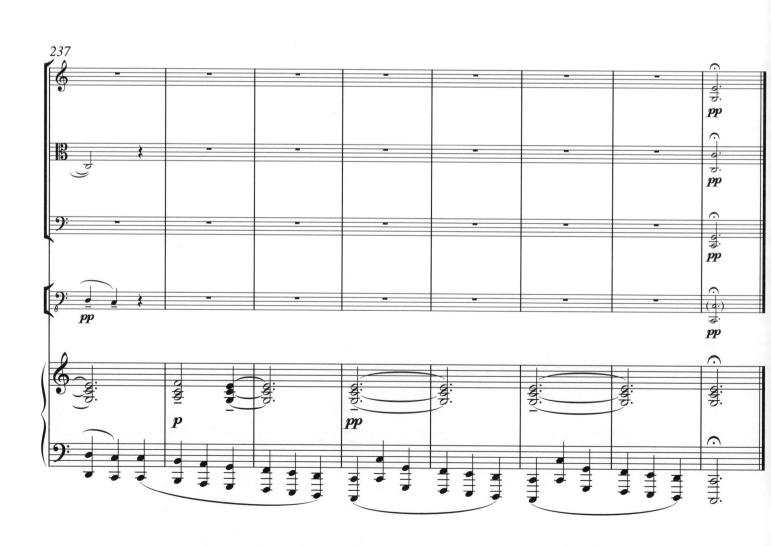